BEWDLEY'S
PAST
IN PICTURES
Vol. 1

BY
KENNETH HOBSON
AND
CHARLES & ANGELA PURCELL

INTRODUCTION

The photographs in the following pages were, in the main, culled from those appearing in Bewdley Civic Society's Exhibition, held in Bewdley Library in June 1993. There are one, or two, notable additions kindly brought to the authors notice whilst the Exhibition was in progress and, thus, too late to be included amongst those then on display.

This volume is intended to be the first of two. It is hoped that the long suffering public will be prepared to find room on their bookshelves for this sort of Bewdleyana. The proceeds (such as they will be) will be applied to the funds of the publishers, the Bewdley Historical Research Group - part of the Bewdley Museum Society, a registered charity.

"Bewdley's Past in Pictures" is intended to reach not only local historians, but, everyone who has lived in, or visited, the town. For a more erudite volume the reader should refer to "Bewdley in its Golden Age" (Life in Bewdley 1660-1760), published by the Bewdley Historical Research Group in 1991, or "Essays towards a History of Bewdley" reprinted in the 1980s by Wyre Forest District Council Museum Service.

The authors would like to thank all those who, in any way, have contributed towards this book, and particularly, those who lent material. Their names are listed elsewhere.

The discovery of all textual, or factual, errors, should be reported to the Chairman of Research Group. So far as the pictures are concerned, there is an old saying - the camera does not lie.

Bewdley 1993

Kenneth Hobson
Charles Purcell
Angela Purcell

BEWDLEY HISTORICAL RESEARCH GROUP

Started in 1981 as a part of Bewdley Museum Society, the Group consists of a small number of people, not all Bewdley residents, who meet once a week, during the winter months to study and extract details relating to the history of Bewdley from historical documents and records. Field work is carried out during the summer months and, so far, this has involved the recording of inscriptions on memorial stones in the local graveyards. Both winter and summer meetings are interspersed with visits to properties of architectural, or , historic interest.

Large quantities of documentary material on Bewdley, Ribbesford, Wribbenhall and Dowles is being collected, produced and stored. The Group's technical aids include the use of a computer, microfilm readers and microfiche scanner. But, in the main, the pen pushers predominate.

A surprisingly large number of enquiries are received by the Group from genealogists, both in this country and abroad, concerning their antecedents with Bewdley connections, all of which are answered with an increasing amount of detail, as more data comes into the Group's archives from the work of the researchers.

A well received history, covering the years 1660-1670, entitled "Bewdley in its Golden Age" was recently published by the Group in hardback form and copies are still available from the group's headquarters at 8 Ironside Close, Bewdley, DY12 2HX, at £10.95 plus £1.50 postage and packing.

The Group is non profit making - all receipts being ploughed back into research or the dissemination of information on Bewdley's history.

BEWDLEY CIVIC SOCIETY

In 1944, before the Second World War had ended, a number of far sighted and optimistic Bewdley residents decided to create the Civic Society. They were far sighted because they could sense that they lived in a fine historic town, of a kind which after the war, might well be in danger, not from enemy action, but from more subtle threats; and they were optimistic, because, at that particular time, it was by no means clear that the War would end in a British victory.

Now, the Society has become what is probably the second largest amenity society in Worcestershire. Its aims are not only to conserve what is good in the town, but to promote interest in it. Thus the Society's activities include visual displays. It was one of these that acted as a catalyst in the creation of this book. A very successful exhibition of photographs entitled "Old Bewdley in Focus", which left the organisers in no doubt that there was tremendous public interest in that aspect of Bewdley's past - and not only in the distant past, but the comparatively recent. Sometimes, during the exhibition, there were more people gathered around a group photograph taken in the fifties than any other picture, the characters appearing in the photograph being the subject of animated discussion. There will be more such displays by the Society.

CONTENTS

FIRST PUBLISHED 1993
COPYRIGHT C. 1993
BEWDLEY HISTORICAL RESEARCH GROUP
ALL RIGHTS RESERVED

British Library Cataloguing Data:
Bewdley's Past in Pictures vol. 1
1. Hereford and Worcester. Bewdley, History
Bewdley Historical Research Group
942.4'49

Printed in Great Britain by
Windmill Printing (1981) Ltd., Portersfield Road, Cradley Heath.

)05. The Summer House can be seen in the distance. Built for William Harwood in 1740
extended in the mid 1800s by the Sturge family who were prominent Quakers.

nuary 1891. The building in the centre is the Chocolate Factory. So damaged by fire in 1968
t it had to be demolished; originally built by Mr. Sturge as Bewdley's answer to the
lderminster carpet factories. It failed as such.

January 1891. Taken from the bottom of Dog Lane.

There was such a hard frost in the winter of 1895 that the Severn (normally a very fast flowing river) was frozen solid, for weeks, and to such an extent that it was possible to have an ox roast under the bridge arches. We are looking at Severn Side North.

ember 1910. On the left of the group is Dr. Thomas Pennington, who lived at Ivy Cottage,
ibbenhall. Note the number of advertisements for bicycles.

ember 1910. One of the few photographs now remaining of the Gas Works; or to give its
I title – The Bewdley Gas Works Co. Ltd.

December 1910. Severn Side North, again, with the George Hotel landing stage well afloat.

"FLOOD". BEWDLEY. JAN.4. 1925.

This century there have, so far, been five very severe floods; 1910, 1925, 1946, 1947 and 1963 each occasioned by heavy snowfall in Wales and Shropshire, followed by a sudden thaw.

...ving a bit of fun, rowing outside number 70 Load Street, then the house and surgery of "Bob" Miles. Now a solicitors.

47. Lax Lane with a house called "Palma", Stourport Road in the background. Demolished 1991 when the Mill House development took place.

1947. Beales Corner or "Venetian Bewdley", photographed from a boat.

1947. The Council weren't flooded with enquiries that day! Number Five is now a ladies fashion shop, bearing that name.

7.

1963. Note the sawmill and tannery on Severn Side South. H.C. Styles' mill is to the right of the picture, with Lax Lane in the foreground.

c.1895. Shows the Severn Side North quayside after the quay wall was built. The Medical Centre now stands on the site of the building to the right of the photograph.

August 25th 1887. Shows Severn Side North before the quay wall was built. Notice Bewdl Floating Swimming Baths in front of the toll house.

1900. Park Lodge, where Richard Hemingway, solicitor, and his family lived. Occupied in 1920 by Daniel Clarke, solicitor. The lawn has gone; it now forms the site of Park Close, off Park Lane. The roof of Tickenhill can just be seen.

1920. Springhill Farm land in the distance, owned by Mr. Reginald Dalley and sold to the Borough Council for the development of the Spring Hill Rise housing estate. Taken before any of the houses in Wheatcroft Avenue (in foreground) were built.

1930s. Charles Rodman Pritchard, several times Mayor of Bewdley, and Samuel Rowe, the Borough Surveyor, surveying land earmarked for the Bark Hill housing estate. The house in the background is Windy Ridge, on the corner of Dry Mill Lane.

c.1905. The Redthorne, built in 1765 by William Prattinton. On his death it passed to his son the antiquarian, Dr. Peter Prattinton. It remained in the Prattinton family until 1865. Now a Rest Home. The picture illustrates the loss of greenery to car parking.

...ese cottages on Wyre Hill, photographed in 1965, were subsequently demolished for the ...rest Close development.

...ese timber-framed buildings on Wyre Hill were restored by the Hereford and Worcester ...lding Preservation Trust as recently as 1992. Of late 15th century construction they were ...e the home and workshop of the Birch family, basket and besom makers.

c.1920. In the foreground is the land on which the Garden Cinema was built on Riverside North about 1921. The first proprietor was Mark Round. Bridge House now stands there.

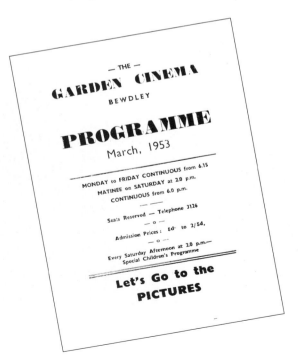

. Sandy Bank leading down into Welch Gate. The cottages were demolished in the 1930s.
small building was used as a butchers.

c.1865. Welch Gate with the Roundabout House and the turnpike gate. The proprietor of the Anchor Inn at this time was John Pountney. Note the baskets hanging outside Samuel Roge shop. Note also the barbers pole.

c.1915. Catchem's End. The corner building was a shop.

15. Kidderminster Road with the house, Lansdowne, on the right. The house on the left of picture carried an advertisement for Sunlight soap.

timber-framed house on the right, altered in the 1920s was the warehouse of Benjamin erell, pewtersmith, and previously of the Beale family after whom the corner was named. four-storey building on the opposite corner is also thought to have belonged to the Beale ly. Victoria House, seen beyond Cotterell's warehouse was built in 1735.

Shows what is now number 16 Kidderminster Road. The timber-framed houses in the centr
once a post office with a member of the Bishop family as postmaster, were demolished to ma
way for the school playground.

c.1910. Stourport Road. The house on the extreme right (no. 117) was built for her head
gardener by Mrs. Wakeman-Newport of Sandbourne.

10. Severn Terrace, Wribbenhall. The row of houses in the centre are thought to be the ...st in Bewdley. They were built in the 14th century. Severn House can just be seen behind ...s on the right. The chimney of Lowe's ropeworks is also visible.

920. A traffic-free view of Load Street from St. Anne's church tower.

c.1912. At the top of the Golden Valley, taken on the wedding day of Tom and Annie Darkes.

e Whitcombe family. Philip and Constance Whitcombe with their children Mildred and
win in the garden of Eversley, Bark Hill.

898. Vera Murdoch's grandparents, Alfred and Elizabeth Hinton, are depicted here. He was
arpenter and Vera can remember watching him make coffins to order. The family lived in a
ttage now replaced by Eastham Court, Severn Side South.

1891. Miss Latter, the governess to the Whitcombe children at Kateshill.

1891. Miss Latter's room at Kateshill.

e Whitcombe family at the rear of 70 Load Street. R.M. and P.W. Whitcombe practiced as
icitors here. Later it was used by Dr. Miles as his surgery.

920. Tom White and his family. He was a timber feller and coal merchant who lived on
re Hill.

c.1865. From an ambrotype negative. Possibly John Smith, brassfounder, and his family, wh
lived at 13 Severn Side South. He was a member of the G.T. Smith family who owned and r
the brass foundry in Load Street.

a party in the garden of Sandbourne photographed by Mrs. Louise Wakeman-Newport, owner, c.1890. Her husband, Henry, is in the centre, with his dogs nearby.

910. J. White, who took this photograph, often used members of his family to pose. The al spans of Dowles railway bridge were removed in 1963.

c.1910. The Grammar School in the Park. The earliest mention of a school is in the
Bridgewardens Account Book for 1577. In 1599 William Monnox, a tanner, left £6 per ann
in his estate "For maintenance of the Free Grammar School". The date on the building is 16
The headmaster was always a clergyman of the Church of England.

c.1900. The Grammar School in High Street which replaced the building in the Park. It wa
built in 1861 on land previously occupied by the Blue Ball Inn. Designed by Henry Day of
Worcester and built of brick with Bath stone facing. The first headmaster was Rev. William
Grist. The school closed in 1912.

910. The Palace School occupied Tickenhill Manor House, off Park Lane, for a few years from c.1900-1920.

30. Children at Wyre Hill Mission School with their teacher Mrs. Dixon. Albert Ward is in the back row. This Home Mission school was built in 1868 and the first known mistress was Miss Pountney. Following the school's closure in 1950 some pupils went to Wribbenhall C of E Primary School and others to Lax Lane School. Afterwards, the building was occupied by Telford Press.

1930/1. Wribbenhall C of E School class.

1938. Wribbenhall C of E School class.

00. Children at Lax Lane National School. Built in 1830 and closed at the end of 1967.
laced by St. Anne's C of E School on Wyre Hill.

1862. Taken during the building of Bewdley Railway Station. The Severn Valley Railway v
officially opened in 1862 and the inaugural journey included Bewdley's M.P. Sir Thomas
Winnington.

Navvies working on the track of the Severn Valley Railway at the Kidderminster end of
Bewdley Station.

am rail-motor at Bewdley Station. John Marshall's book, "The Severn Valley Railway" ions that these vehicles were in operation on that railway from 1905 until 1918. At first, een Kidderminster, Bewdley and Stourport and, later, between Hartlebury, Stourport and lley, as well. The steam engine was incorporated within the single coach. They could get o Bewdley from Kidderminster in ten minutes and from Bewdley to Stourport in seven.

0. A brougham in the George Hotel yard. This vehicle regularly plied between the hotel 3ewdley Station at this time. The brougham was named after Sir Henry Peter Brougham olitician and educational reformer.

c.1910. Outside the George Hotel. The George Hotel was one of the important posting hou from whence carriages left for Birmingham and London.

A horse brake outside the George Hotel, used for carrying passengers and luggage between the hotel and the station.

September 1938. Miss Halford of Hill Farm, Northwood, in the foreground with her ber-tyred milk float.

12. Miss Kathleen Marks, nanny to the children of J.H. Cooper, proprietor of the George :el, with her charges.

c.1910. Premises of Samuel Tudge, blacksmith, who took over from his father John, who ha
moved from Park Lane in 1861.

00. Premises in Dog Lane of James Tudge, blacksmith and farrier. He was the cousin of uel Tudge of High Street. The "X" marks the position of the Dog Lane gate.

orge Lawley's smithy at the corner of Northwood Lane (formerly Rag Lane) and lderminster Road. The Lawley family operated from here from c.1860.

c.1910. The Bewdley Borough Fire Brigade outside the Guildhall. This was their headquarte
until the present Fire Station was built in 1960. In 1908 Harry Evans was the "foreman" of t
brigade. The earliest reference to a Bewdley fire "engine" was 1709 when it was kept in the
church.

1960. The first practice of the fire brigade at their new station between Load Street and Dog
Lane. The Station was formally opened by Cllr. Mrs Florence Pritchard. High ranking Coun
firemen are looking on.

horseless carriage outside Winterdyne. For many years the house was occupied by Giles
haw, the brother-in-law of Frances Ridley Havergal, the famous hymn writer.

1910. Model T Ford at the George Hotel with a figure who closely resembles Tom Gardner.

c.1934. Cars in Winbrook. The houses in the centre were later demolished.

1947. A Post Office van negotiating the flood water at Beales Corner.

ewdley's steam fire engine was used as a pump when laying water pipes under the river. lere, she is being towed to work by a lorry.

here was this outing from? Bewdley must have wondered what was happening. Note the rt of Bewdley Gas company on the left. The Gas Works were erected on the west bank of e river at Dowles in 1837, and the town was first lit by gas in January 1838.

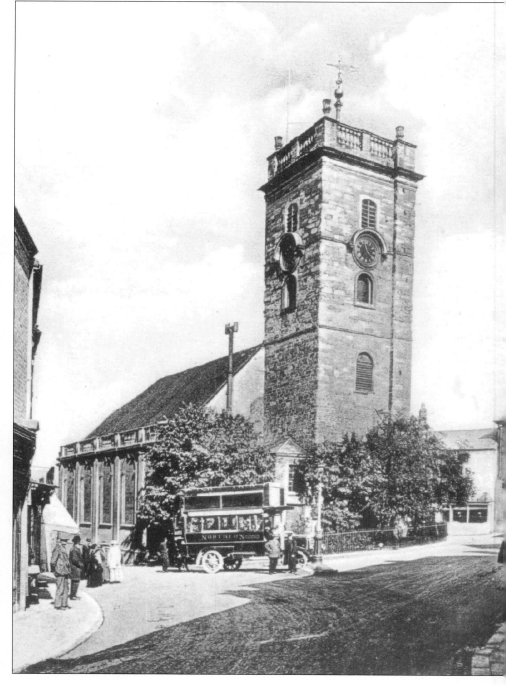

An omnibus of the Northern Company parked outside St. Anne's church. Was it on an outing? Note the railings around the church. These remained until the 1950s.

917 Midland Red experimented with gas-powered buses as an economy measure. The coal store was near the Kidderminster Town Hall and each supply enabled the bus to travel 8 es.

947 Midland Red bus negotiating the floodwaters at Beales Corner with Severn Side South he background.

Solid tyred vehicle outside the George Hotel in Load Street laden with pipes for work on the Elan Valley-Birmingham aqueduct supplement. Thought to be about 1912.

c.1942. Harold Carter with his milk delivery van. He started work in March 1917, at the age 13½, at Lowe's Rope Works in Wribbenhall. J.P. Thomas began as a dairy farmer at Heath Farm, Wribbenhall. Working for a short time from Load Street, then, until 1962, from 21 Stourport Road retailing and delivering milk.

ws a trow, or wherry, tied up in front of Victoria House, Stourport Road. The house was
t in 1735. The mid 18th century warehouses on the right became H.C. Styles, corn
chants.

en trows, or wherries, moored at Severn Side South. Seen from Stourport Road.

S.S. Amo, from Stourport, at Severn Side South near the bridge. Boats of this size could or reach Bewdley when the river was very high.

The Arley Castle, or the Fairy Queen, dressed overall for a Carnival, with Severn Side Sou in the background. In either case, the vessels were horsedrawn. The Bank on the right was established by Samuel Skey and later became the Midland Bank, and occupied as such between 1832 and 1967.

Caravan Park, Bewdley

8798

)s. Note the variety of vehicles used as holiday homes.

l barge of Thomas Gardner junior, a coal and timber merchant and general haulier, who
l at 28 Severn Side South. The first reference to a Thomas Gardner in the town records is
878.

c.1910. The Running Horse, Long Bank, licensee Arthur Hall. The inn, formerly called the Waggon & Horses and the Horse & Jockey became the Running Horse by 1857.

c.1905. The Black Boy at Wyre Hill. This is thought to be a 15th century building, restored the 19th and 20th centuries. The Inn was known as the Black Boy by 1817 and was occupi by William Pountney. The other cottages are mostly of late 17th and early 18th century dat

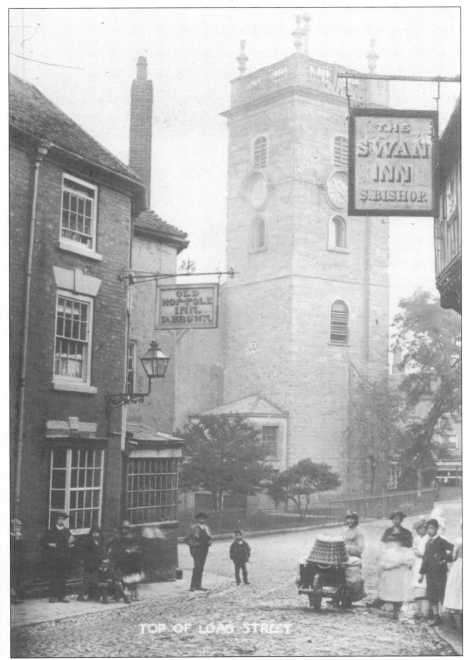

65. The Old Hop Pole is now numbers 45 and 46 Load Street. The building is of early
century origin. but was refronted in the mid 18th century. The proprietor, David Brown,
also a butcher. The Swan was also a 16th century building but was completely rebuilt.
Susan Bishop was the licensee until at least 1896.

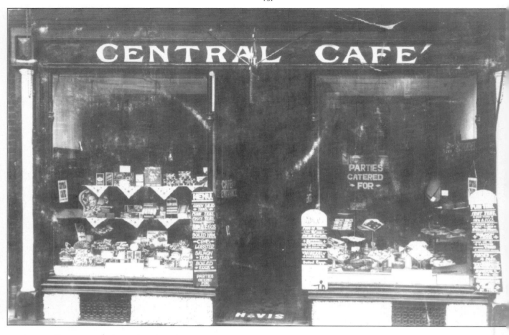

c.1930. The Central Café, Load Street as it was in its heyday. The building, now the Co-operative, is of early 17th century origin. The present frontage was added in the 1980s.

1980s. The Central Café before alterations.

side the George Hotel. This 17th century building was originally known as The Sign of
t George in 1706 and was occupied by Thomas Burlton. It stayed in the Burlton family
c.1777. It was known as the George Inn by 1709. There was a bowling green at the rear
this was where Bewdley Bowling Club started.

interesting that as late as 1912 reference was still being made to posting horses, as seen in
photograph. The horses were, probably, actually used to draw wagonettes and passenger-
ying vehicles, or hired out.

1938. The Angel Hotel being demolished, to be rebuilt further back from the street. The building seen here is of mock timber-framing. The original building, of early 17th century d. became the Angel Inn in 1694. Herbert Parman was the licensee at the time of the demolitio and the brewery was Mitchells and Butlers.

1960s. The Chocolate Box was a confectioners and coffee shop. It closed in the late 1960s, becoming the Midland Bank. The property was built in 1776, and, during the Second Worl War the first floor was used as a canteen for troops; run by volunteers.

70s. The Wheatsheaf. This photograph was taken by Joseph Humphreys, photographer, who was also a watchmaker and jeweller. From the late 18th century the Wheatsheaf was one of the main posting houses of Bewdley with coaches calling morning and night from Birmingham and London, as well as more local areas. The proprietor at the time of the photograph was William Blount. The building was converted into a "Science & Arts Institute" in the 1870s and at one time part of it was used as the Bewdley Coffee Tavern, established by a Temperance Society.

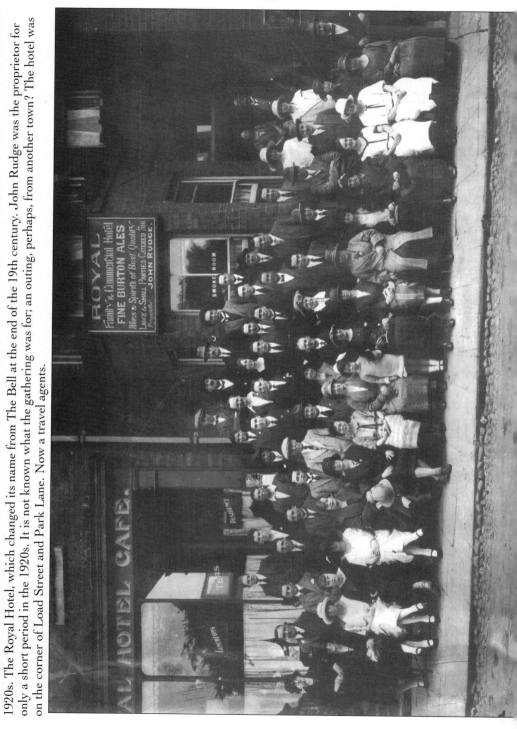

1920s. The Royal Hotel, which changed its name from The Bell at the end of the 19th century. John Rudge was the proprietor for only a short period in the 1920s. It is not known what the gathering was for; an outing, perhaps, from another town? The hotel was on the corner of Load Street and Park Lane. Now a travel agents.

1905. The King's Head, 60 High Street, was run at this time by Frederick Martin, who was
[al]so the proprietor at the Pack Horse lower down High Street. The children with the basket of
[wa]shing are the daughters of Samuel Tudge, blacksmith, of 67 High Street. The man with the
[lon]g white apron is thought to be Mr H. Oakes from Tudges smithy.

[18]97. The Pack Horse in High Street, celebrating Queen Victoria's Jubilee. One of the men is
[kn]own to be Mr Ife, the cellar-man, who lived at 27 High Street. Edward Taylor was the
[pu]blican.

c.1910. The Thurstan Hotel when Miss Nellie Longley was the publican. The building was erected in 1775 for John Patten, a wealthy merchant. It became known as Thurstan House in 1892. Gardner's barge is moored near to the Gardner's premises – 28 Severn Side South.

c.1905. The Great Western from Whispering Street, through the railway arch. The Red Lion on the right, has been known as such since the early 19th century. The publican at the time of the photograph was Mrs. Martha Webb who had been there since 1881. Part of the Red Lion was built in the early 18th century.

916. Formerly known as the Rifleman Inn, The Great Western was so named because of its
se proximity to the Great Western Railway. Frederick James Richards was the publican
m c. 1916-1925.

920s. The Rising Sun on Kidderminster Road. The publican was Harry Giles Perkins who
d been there since 1916.

c.1950. Outside the Snack Bar by the Garden Cinema on the river bank, viewed from Bewdley Bridge.

05. Thomas Hollins, butcher's shop at 25 Load Street. Mr Hollins only appears to have been
these premises from 1904-1906, although his name appeared above the shop for many years
erwards. It then became F. H. Brown's. T. F. Timmis took it over some time before 1914.
e building is of the early 17th century. Now Bewdley Butchers.

910. James Humpherson outside his tobacconist's shop at 72 Load Street. James, who was
o the rate collector, took over the premises in 1884. He remained there until 1925 when his
ighter Adelaide Humpherson became the owner. She was superseded by another daughter,
bella, in 1937.

c.1920. William Palmer, watchmaker, 60 Load Street. He occupied the premises from 1891 until 1937 when John Davies, electrical supplies acquired it. The building is of early 17th century origin refronted in the mid 18th century. The passage to the side shows evidence of timber-framing, as well as a first floor jetty.

0. William Hunt, 40 Load Street, builder and contractor moved down from 63 Wyre Hill,
73 Winbrook in 1900 and then came here in 1903. The business moved to Stourport Road in
1950s. The building is of the early 17th century which was clad in the late 18th century.
w a ladies hairdresser's.

1922. Clarice Mapp on the steps of 29 Load Street. A. E. Mapp was a baker and confectioner
as well as a newsagent, stationer and fancy goods dealer. He also offered a lending library
service. The building is of early 19th century date.

1930. A. E. Mapp's, 29 Load Street.

1910. The corner of High Street with Load Street. At this time Henry Hillier,
rocer, occupied the corner shop which was later to become known as The Borough
tores. Note the sign for the Norwich Union Fire Insurance. At the Talbot Inn, seen
n the right, Mrs Emma Bishop was licensee. Thomas Jenks, hairdresser, next to
e Talbot also sold fishing tackle and repaired umbrellas!

1951. The window display at Bert Grainger's, 68 Load Street, for the Festival of Britain.

ch 1947. "Iris" Grainger on the steps of her shop, 68 Load Street, during the flood.

ns Garage for sale. The petrol was served by swing arms over the pavement to the nozzles.
his time (1968) the garage, although trading under the name of "Evans", was actually
ed by the Blood family. Now Dillons.

For many years the Pleveys were the town's leather merchants, carrying on business at number 46 Load Street, just where Load Street curves round, before becoming Welch Gate. Mr Birt Plevey is in the centre of this photograph. Over the years the family also had shops 17 Dog Lane and 64 Load Street.

shop window to number 55 Load Street, c.1905. In turn, the owners have been Joseph
ks, Crookes, E. M. Forster, E. Palmer and M. Hadley. After a century of chemists, the
mises have become established as an eating place, having been variously known as the
ck of Beyond", "The Box of Delights" and "J.R.'s".

p blinds are, unfortunately, not nearly so common a feature of the street scene as they
e. This photograph depicts the row of shops in Load Street, just below the Guildhall, about
0. Dalley occupied the building from the 1940s, as a stationer and printer. Prior to him
. W. Harris, H. G. Perkins, M. E. Bryan and E. P. Shepherd, all stationers and printers,
led from here.

Now the "L'Ile de France", number 61 Load Street. Walter Styles was for many years one of the town's chemists. A member of the very well known Styles family, he died in tragic circumstances. In 1708 the building was known as the Red Lyon Inn (previously The Ship). Just in picture is Harcombe's which stocked a vast range of goods, ranging from household linen to bedsocks.

A. Dudfields, the ironmongers, number 58 Load Street, decorated for Queen Victoria's
bilee in 1897. Mr. Dudfield committed suicide on the premises about 1900. In the 1950s the
ade of the building was found to be unsafe and Wrensons, the then owners, commissioned a
uild, but, in a Georgian style.

Load Street, by the side of St. Anne's Church about 1870, when the street was cobbled. Nov
Jackson's, butcher, the shop was a butchers back to the 1830s. The man featured here in his
white coat is possibly John Potter, butcher. The shop on the extreme left, had previously bee
part of Richard Plevey's, saddler, and before him Thomas Griffiths, also a saddler.

Load Street, Miss Lynes shop. She dispensed stationery and was officially sanctioned to
ix embossed stamps to papers and documents – an essential part of trading at one time. The
ved shop front has been saved and is now in Bewdley Museum.

WRIBBENHALL

POST OFFICE

WRIBBENHALL POST OFFICE

The Post Office in Whispering Street, c.1905, just on the corner of the lane leading past Chr'
Church lych gate. What would one give for a really close look at the postcard views of
Bewdley which are on sale. This building is one of the few in Bewdley displaying a firemark.
Wribbenhall was served, in turn, by three Post Offices. One by the Black Boy, which was
demolished to make the school yard, then this one in Whispering Street, later converted to a
house, and today, one in Kidderminster Road.

other view of Wribbenhall Post Office.

e Old Town Hall on Wyre Hill. For many years, up until the early 1980s, a general store,
t now a private residence. Historians considered, at one time, that Bewdley first became
ablished on Wyre Hill, before the settlement on the riverside. This theory has received a
ere jolt as a result of recent research carried out by Mr Don Gilbert.

All the notables attended the opening of the Parish Room in Wribbenhall, including the Bis
of Worcester, the Rector of Bewdley (Rev. A. H. Moore), Mrs Llewellyn of Severn House,
Dr. Johnston (whose surgery was at Ivy Cottage), Mr. Hunt (builder of the room) and Mis
Cordy Manby, from Wribbenhall House, with her personal maid, Susan. The Manby's prov
ed the funds for the building.

Outside the Old Town Hall on Wyre Hill. Information as to who the party were and why th
were gathered there, would be greatly appreciated.

e 1910 General Election, when Stanley Baldwin successfully defended his seat which he
d just won in an unopposed by-election. But not everyone supported him – notice the
ttelton poster being displayed in a somewhat furtive manner.

tside number 7 Load Street, again in 1910. The "loaf poster" in the shop window was a
erence to one of the burning questions of the day – free trade, or not. The two loaves were
bolic of the suggestion that the imposition of a tariff on imported corn would not
essarily result in an increase in the cost of living. Mrs Darkes sports the large hat.

The Bewdley Territorials off to war. The horrific casualty lists, a feature of the First World War, were then in the future. As one can see, the occasion was a light-hearted affair. They would be home by Christmas!

Harold Carter, who loaned these photographs, recalls that, of the soldiers shown in this picture, nine out of ten did not return.

sil Night in St. George's Hall in the twenties. Did other towns, as well as Bewdley, hold
sil Nights, raising money for the elderly? The balcony can be seen, which sadly, although it
exists, is now closed off.

George's Hall, next to the car park in Load Street, laid up for tea. The lace tablecloths con-
trast strongly with the sturdy cups. One wonders whether the chairs stacked as readily as
those used today.

A motor cycle rally starting in Load Street, c.1922. A popular form of enjoyment amongst th
more daring well-to-do. The ladies travelled by side-car, as seen in the top right of the pictur

What is now the car park entrance can be seen as part of Jenks's Garage. Number 67 becar
Barclays Bank in 1940, but then was a doctor's house. Amongst the riders was Cecil
Hemingway, local solicitor.

e rally ends at Hernes Nest House, with tea on the tennis court. Miss Kate Tangye, who
d there, being a keen motorist.

en they were all photographed! Cecil is by the side of Mayor Green (his uncle by marriage)
n the left of the second row.

It was the custom, should the local clergy marry, whilst in office, to decorate the village, for return of the incumbent and his bride from their honeymoon. This and the following six vie show Wribbenhall decorated, as a welcome to Canon Reginald Chesshire's bride. The pictu afford fine views of the local streets and some well known buildings. The sequence termina at the vicarage – Storridge House in Kidderminster Road, now an Accountant's offices.

cene, showing Severn Side South, during the first post-war carnival, 1946, when Marjorie
ainger (nee Bradbury) was Queen.

The Cherry Market in Load Street, just below St. Anne's Church. Fred Harvatt can recall being paid sixpence per day to look after a stall holder's donkey whilst the market was on. Sometimes, the market extended into Cole's yard in Dog Lane. Cherries were brought down for sale from Far Forest and Hales Park.

In Gardner's Meadow, behind the backs of the houses in Lower Park. The Bewdley Girl Guides inauguration in 1924, with girls from other Guide groups joining in. Mayoress, Mrs J. H. Cooper is in the picture.

In 1910 a horse drawing a Kidderminster butcher's trap, with three people on board, bolted into the river at the spot marked "X". It also carried the weekend takings from his shop, mair in sovereigns.

The butcher was thrown out before the trap entered the water. The lady passenger was drowned, but the boy, shown here with his rescuers, was saved.

...sent at the award ceremony, thought to have been in the Angel, was Cecil Hemingway, T D ...ter and Stanley Baldwin. Boy and rescuers are at the back, right.

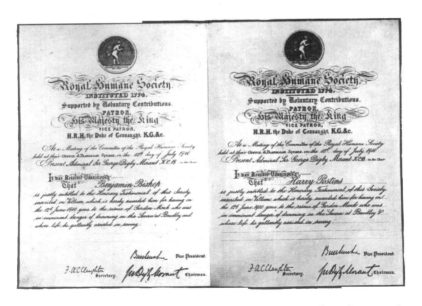

...e award certificates, or, at least, two of them. The third rescuer, for whom we do not have a ...tificate, was Mr Ainsworth.

Rosenhurst, viewed from Park Lane, about 1902. The house collapsed in the 1970s as a resu
of nearby building work, during the course of construction of houses in Telford Drive. Own
over the years have included Langley Kitching, Whittington Langdon and Mr Fred Mills.

·k Lane in 1965, showing Orchard House, the home of the Coldrick family. Removed as
t of the road widening scheme to make way for Orchard Rise.

ught in the act! The demolition contractor at work on the School Hall in Park Lane, about
57. This was part of the Borough Council road widening scheme. It has to be admitted that
s part of Park Lane was narrow, but so are other parts today.

How narrow Park Lane was, is shown in this picture of three other properties which were demolished for the road improvement scheme, with the timber-framed Capper's Cottage in middle.

In Load Street in 1965, looking west. The bottom of Park Lane can be seen at the top left, with the shop facing Load Street (no. 34) and the three properties behind it, all removed for road widening. Parked cars now replace them! The building in the centre is of early 17th century construction and has an elaborate plaster ceiling on the first floor. The decorative rainwater head is inscribed "1722/LR".

view of Load Street looking west from the bridge. On the right, a building with a steeply
ched roof (no. 69) which might have been timber-framed and which was replaced by the
esent building in Victorian times. Now Griffith's shop.

ttages in the Hollow (at the bottom of Richmond Road) which were demolished in the thir-
. Number 117 Richmond Road is on the left.

The "Coffin House" in Dog Lane. So called, because of its wedge shape. There is now mere triangular-shaped piece of grass to indicate its existence. The home of the Sedgeley family a many years before, owned by one of the Coldrick family.

ig before their demolition in the fifties, one of these buildings held a licence and was known
he Dog Wheel Inn. In 1887 Edward Plevey, the publican, was licensed to "let post-horses,
s, cabs & broughams". In Dog Lane, but a little nearer to Welch Gate than the Coffin
use.

Severn Side South. T. H. Williams' saw yard and timber store. After removal, the site was an
irritation to conservationists, being used as a second-hand car lot. Now Old Tannery Court.
The lone lady is Mrs Taylor.

A 1950s view of all the buildings which were levelled in Severn Side South. Their replace-
ments being, Severn Quay, Telford Court, Old Tannery Court and Eastham Court.

gh Street looking north at the turn of the century. One can just glimpse the timbers of num-
57 which now provides an access to Burlton's Terrace.

The Bridge Toll House, or Round House, which stood at one side of Telford's Bridge and formed part of the original design. One likes to think that, had its fate hung in the balance now, instead of in 1960, then it would not have been pulled down. Used as a shop, many people alive today can recall buying sweets there from Mrs Gale. It extended two floors do to river level.

Economics, not floodwaters, decided the fate of the Garden Cinema. The building there now just by the Bridge, on Riverside North, is called Bridge House. The river water interrupted showings of "Murder in Reverse", with William Hartnell.

ne time the main (Kidderminster) road into the town was only some 12 feet wide by the
ck Boy, in Wribbenhall. The road wound around the garden wall to Wribbenhall House
n here, behind the trees in the centre of the picture). In the thirties the house (originally
t by a pewterer) was demolished and the County Council took the opportunity of popping
Police Station and some police houses in its garden.

e local authority had just got into its stride with a "slum clearance" scheme for Whispering
eet and had already knocked down the old Bullhouses in 1938 when, fortunately, the
ond World War intervened and no more old houses in the street were lost. Every war cloud
a silver lining.

Little can be recalled of the cottages at the rear of the Great Western, their loss (if such it be
is too recent. Kidderminster Road can just be glimpsed between the tree and the rear of num
ber 40.

St. Andrew's Church, Dowles, demolished in 1956. Standing one meadow away from the riv
traces of the graveyard are still there, or what has been left to us by the vandals. Built in 178
of brick, it suffered from lack of use for at least 20 years before the decision was made to pul
down. There are signs of a deserted medieval village nearby. This is an early photograph.

s picture of Joseph Mobberley, the cattle drover, in Welch Gate, also shows the small ghbridge building near the junction of Sandy Bank. Joe and his wife Charlotte were often e seen taking cattle through the streets and they frequently had fierce quarrels, which often ne to blows. Woe betide anyone who intervened. Both Charlotte and Joe could then, justifi-y, vent their joint anger on the stranger.

rn gathering and sheep shearing at Blackstone Farm. The barn still stands, a little off to the e of the Bewdley to Stourport Road. The telegraph poles follow the line of the road. egraphy was generally introduced in, or about, 1890, so this picture might be dated 1900.

The Snuff Mill in the Golden Valley c.1910. Very little now remains of the old mill, once owned by "Snuffy" Holder, just the odd piece of timber and some bricks. It stood by the bro which runs through the bottom of the Park, thence through St. Anne's House garden and th Old Rectory; under Lax Lane and then into the river.

Besom-making on Wyre Hill by two members of the Bishop family, one of whom laboured under the nickname "Coddy". Bewdley was ideally suited for the manufacture of besoms, wit the Wyre Forest close at hand for materials and ready markets, in the shape of Birmingham and the Black Country, lying to the east.

...umber of Tom Gardner's family are here, resting for a moment from their labours in ...kworks Meadow, on the riverside towards Dowles. He had with him, Amy Doolittle, Elsie ...dner, Emily and Blanche Crutchley and Beatrice Postins.

...Tower Farm, Long Bank, a mile or two west of Bewdley, loading hay. In a row from left to ...t, Richard Bond, Ernest Wilson, George Pound, Thomas Pound and Harvey Bond. On ...of the hay, George Townsend. Until 1993 the Pound family owned Tower Farm.

Home Farm barns, Ribbesford, c.1920. The main barn, nearest Ribbesford Church, has owl holes in the gable ends and bears a stone coat of arms, the building being of considerable age built in the 17th century. Inside, it has a cathedral-like quality.

In the twenties, the road through Home Farm past the barns and thence to Ribbesford House was not tree-lined, as it is today. Just a clump of walnut trees, away to the left.

bark harvest, coming down from Wyre Forest. There were, at one time, many tanneries in ·dley and oak bark was an essential ingredient in the tanning process. George Harrison, on right of this picture, was later drowned on the day of the first carnival. The horses came n Hunt's stables, some of which were at the rear of what is now number 4 Welch Gate and ·rs at the rear of number 39 Load Street.

·re bark peel, outside its destination – the tannery on Severn Side South – in the twenties.

Douglas Grainger's father, Bert, is breaking in a young horse at Lightmarsh Farm using a specially made cart, designed so that the colt could not kick backwards. Later, Bert became owner of a greengrocery business at 68 Load Street – now the Photographic Shop.

Elliott and Roger Page working with a seed driller at Hoarstone Farm, about 1920, in the fie by the road to Trimpley. Both were big men and, farmed Hoarstone from the twenties until t late sixties. Sue Healey, who now lives in the farmhouse saved this and many other photos o the farm, for us to see.

er-making near the Button Oak road. The cider juice can be seen running out of the press,
ing been squeezed through the horsehair mats.

ese Bewdley ladies are making whisks from birch twigs. Once made into bunches they were
d locally in the carpet industry for removing "flights", or fluff, from the carpet. The craft
ried on in a small way in the Wyre Forest until the 1970s.

Wribbenhall Men's Swimming Club, c.1930. There was no hesitation, in those days, about swimming in the river Severn. In the back row, from left to right, are Viv Whitmore, Ernest Poulton, Ronald Bond, Clarence Stokes and Tug Wilson. In the front row – Gordon Baldw Harold Simmonds and Sydney Bayliss. All of them Wribbenhall residents.

Bewdley Ladies Gymnastic Club, 1907, with their instructor, Dick Lowe. No smile appears his face – but he should be happy with 19 young ladies in his care. Perhaps he was keeping wary eye on those Indian Clubs!

Company Bewdley Riflemen, of the First Volunteer Battalion of of the Worcester regiment, 5, under the command of Major R.H. Whitcombe, proudly displaying their scores in the oting competition. Many Bewdley names appear on the blackboard.

hard Perrin's picture of the Bewdley Rowing Club at Beales Corner near the bridge. The b was founded in 1877.

Originally the Rowing Club's headquarters comprised a raft moored at Beales Corner, near spot where this photograph was taken, c.1925, 200 yards downstream from the bridge. The present clubhouse was erected in 1961.

After the race, c.1925. Framed by one of the bridge arches, one can just make out a large advertisement for the latest attraction at the Garden Cinema.

ck Strange by the Rowing Club raft. c.1930.

The house behind the Bewdley Scout Group has not been identified and the authors would welcome suggestions.

The Bewdley Bible Class Football team at Kateshill, Lower Park, c.1900. Mr. R. H. Whitcom is with them. Unfortunately for the researcher (and our editors), there were two Robert He Whitcombe's, father and son, and it is not always easy to tell which was which.

The Mug House Fishing Club. The sign over the Inn, which is still on Severn Side North, mentions the name of the proprietor, and states that he is "late of Birmingham". Clearly, the licensee was proud of his Birmingham background, and so he should have been! Doubtless the many visitors from Brum to Bewdley would have been encouraged by the information that their host was one of them.

The Reverend John Burton, headmaster, with the Grammar School cricketers. His books on the histories of Bewdley and Kidderminster are still great sources of reference. By his side are, at the back, W. Booth, Mears, H. James and W. Betts. In the front row, John Tangye, John Betts, C. J. Grist, Stanley Hemingway, Herbert Dunn, P. W. Whitcombe, Albert Tangye, N. Other, Gurney and Dick Ransom.

Alderman H. N. Frost had the honour of being allowed the first serve at the opening of Bewdley Tennis Club's courts in Stourport Road, c.1924.

wdley Comrades Football Club and their supporters, including Mayor J. H. Cooper, on the ps of St. George's Hall in 1924. The Comrades were formed by ex-servicemen of the First orld War. Previously, Bewdley footballers played under the name of "Bewdley Vics".

Bewdley Bowling Club at Hadley Green, 1906, the year the Club was founded. It started behind the George Hotel in Load Street, where the George now has its car park. At one , every self respecting pub had its own bowling green. The Club moved to its present site, g Riverside North, in 1957.

A mixed hockey group, including E. Cecil Hemingway, about 1910.

Constance and Philip Whitcombe playing croquet on the lawn at Kateshill, Lower Park.

wdley Bandstand was erected in 1921 on Severn Side South as a result of fund raising by
Bewdley and Wribbenhall Brass Band Society. When Mr. Mark Round opened the
rden Cinema that year, proceeds from the first performance were donated to the Bandstand
d. Bewdley Borough Council removed the roof (to save the expense of repairing it) in, or
ut, 1965.

Queen Victoria's Golden Jubilee in 1897 being celebrated in Load Street.

Initially, there were five men from Bewdley in the E. Battalion who volunteered for service in South Africa at the start of the Boer War (1899-1902). Here they are, photographed in South Africa, with Major (then Captain) R. H. Whitcombe. They are believed to include, L/Cpl. Harry Darkes and Private Ernest Moles.

e Bewdley Five returned home safely in 1902 and, here, preparations are being made at the
ildhall in Load Street for their welcome.

ero's welcome for the Bewdley Five; Load Street crowded with girls leaning out of
dows and standing on any flat roof which was available.

The 1910 Mayor's Sunday was well recorded. This and the next two illustrations covered it. There are more scenes, snapped by the same photographer, in other collections. Here, the procession is passing number 1 Load Street, now Teddy Grays, but then Hinton's shop.

In this scene, the 1910 Mayor's Sunday procession is about to enter St. Anne's Church, in Load Street. Hollins butcher's shop is in the background. A more detailed picture of this sho appears earlier, in the "Shops" section.

art of the crowd at the 1910 Mayor's Sunday. Padmore's shop in the background. Now the hicular entrance to the rear of the Old Post Office in Load Street.

lebrations for the Coronation of King George V., in 1911; some very exotic instruments in e band. With Mayor Green outside the Guildhall.

Outside the entrance to St. Anne's Church in Load Street. It is not known what occasion warranted a full turn-out of the band. It is assumed that it is the Bewdley Town Band.

Marching along High Street, with Major Whitcombe at the head of the column, just by the Old Grammar School building. Presumably marching around the town and thus, shortly abo to turn down into Lax Lane.

...ace celebrations in 1920 (although the First World War armistice was signed in 1918, fight-
...g in Russia, against a different foe, didn't cease until 1919). With the Rowing Club raft and
...e bridge illuminated. The lights consisted of hundreds of candles in small glass jars
...spended by wires. Some appeared on sale a few years ago in a local antique shop.

...urther scene from the 1920 Peace celebrations, outside the bakery at 2 High Street. Jimmy,
... horse, could dance in time to music and was owned by Frank Heydon, the baker.

General de Gaulle, leader of the Free French, taking the salute outside the Guildhall during the Second World War, in 1942 or 1943. The General made a few visits to Bewdley, because Ribbesford House was used for training French officers, being the equivalent St. Cyr abroad France being then under German occupation. Furthermore, the General's son Philippe, was stationed at Ribbesford.

Lower Park House (now flats), on the occasion of the unveiling, in 1955, of a memorial plaque, affixed by Bewdley Civic Society and indicating the birthplace of Stanley Baldwin, Prime Minister, on and off, between 1923 and 1937. The plaque is being unveiled by Lord Cobham. Amongst those watching are Sir Gerald Nabarro, M.P., Alderman Frost, Dr. G. S. Lawrence (Chairman of the Society), Mr. E. J. Wilkins (Secretary), Mrs. Withers and Mr. W. E. James (Mayor).

ncess Alexandra visited Bewdley for the 500th anniversary of the 1472 Charter. Here she is ing to some of the crowd outside the Guildhall in Load Street. A notable triumph was red by Bewdley Museum, which had rushed to be open in time for the Royal visit. A uest was put in by Museum officials for this brand new feature to be included on the ncess's official tour, but this was refused. She was, however, persuaded, without much iculty, to come inside, before she left the Guildhall building.